HOW THE LAW FAILS US
**The People That We Rely On
For Our Protection Can Be
The Biggest Offenders Of It**

I0462368

Table Of Contents

Law Is For Lawyers

Introduction

When there is a glitch in the legal system, lawyers are quick to defend it against all outside derision. They are known to say that the system works, in spite of occasional, glaring, abuses. It 'works', they say, because there is essentially no body with power that will correct the shortcomings so that every user of the law gets a fair shake. It takes a major screw up for a lawyer to be censored or disbarred.

I have a number of friends who are lawyers in various categories, and some of their stories are enough to make a grown person shudder. In addition to these unfortunate tales, their attitudes towards the events do not show much empathy for those who are victimized. *'Oh well'* seems to be a common theme in their thinking. Some clients will win and some clients will lose, but that does not always impact feelings and payday for the lawyers.

Let's face it. Lawyers and judges have an immense amount of power in the court room. Judges especially can make rulings that seriously effect people's lives or livelihood. While someone has to do that job, oversight on their decisions is spotty at best. Short of being overruled by a higher court on rare occasions, they get to say what goes. We have to rely on a judge's good sense and an appropriate application of the law.

From My Perspective

One of the more interesting aspects of law and justice that I have observed on the legal landscape is that the fox is in charge of the chicken coop. The preponderance of lawyers in government results in laws that suit lawyers and the judges (*who are also lawyers*) who rule on laws. Curiously, while they occasionally may be involved with prosecuting conflict of interest cases, they don't seem to be aware of their own conflicted system. Or is it that they don't care to change it?

Some try to justify the preponderance of lawyers in Congress as appropriate since these are people who are making laws. Using that logic, anyone in state and city councils or on homeowner association boards should be a lawyer, because only lawyers can properly have insights and make laws. Does that half-baked train of thought have your approval? A downside to a government full of lawyers is that they come from the privileged class. And what would you think their agenda might be when it involves the wealthy vs. the poor?

Another criticism about lawyers is that they have a disincentive (*conflict of interest*) when it comes to settling cases in an expeditious manner. That is especially prevalent in family disputes where each side may want to punish their opponent as much as possible. Rather than forcefully suggesting mediation or binding arbitration, lawyers may be inclined to let clients unnecessarily run up their legal bills. And of course this behavior can be manifested at the corporate level as well.

Who Is At Fault?

It is obvious that there are numerous and frequent injustices in our legal system. This is not to say that I have any special insight into the legal process that others might not have discovered. It is just that I have experienced the courts firsthand, and have looked at a few of the problems that are symptomatic of a less than perfect manner in which jurisprudence is exercised in this country. What we have is a system that usually works, but has glaring exceptions to the concept of justice. Well, *usually* doesn't get it. When power is pitted against principal, the civil rights of the weak can be subverted in favor of those who have money, status, or connections. This concept is not just a pie-in-the-sky theory, and one I will reflect on.

I recall my 20-something experience with the South Daytona Police Department. After spending time in a dance hall, my friend and I went outside to await the return of the fellow who drove us there. In spite of being both sober and quiet, a clearly red-necked cop pulled up and demanded that we get in the back of his vehicle. Vagrancy was the mumbled excuse. He then proceeded to pick up a buddy and race recklessly through the town. We ended up at the police station, which turned out to be a small converted house with the dispatch in its kitchen. Through some miracle of chance our buddy managed to see what had happened and followed us to the station. When I saw him at the door, my release of nervous tension resulted in near hysterical laughter. To get to the punch line, we were given 24 hours to leave town.

Lawyers Required

Have you tried to secure simple regulatory advice from some city or business office clerk and been told that you needed to contact a lawyer for the answer? Organizations are so afraid of litigation that they won't even discuss aspects of their own business without a warrant.

Or what about doctors who are prevented from revealing information about a deceased patient to the police because lawyers have made sure that they are too intimidated to act on their own? Who says that lawyers make the best judges of fair and reasonable? Even the Attorney General's office in my state will not provide any counseling beyond disclosing the wording of a particular law. So if one wants to comprehend the implications of a law they must either be able to read gibberish to understand the statute, or *(and here's the good part)* hire a lawyer to do so.

In my case I was attempting to determine the statute of limitation on hidden constructions defects. This is hardly a matter to require a lawyer, or so one would might imagine. Lawyers, it appears, are as interested in protecting their sources of income as they are in serving the public good.

The only relief from this unnecessary overhead can sometimes be to file an action in Small Claims court where lawyers are not required. But these matters are restricted to petty cases that are *(duh)* not big revenue producers for lawyers.

Our legal system's lexicon reminds me of the many years when I was a Computer Systems Analyst. Initially I was educated to use obtuse, but exact, jargon when dealing with programming. While many of the terms have become well-known today, words like megabytes, sectors, platters, software, downloading, hardwired, etc. were all alien to most folks. My dad never quite understood what it was that I did for a living.

Lawyers are also egregious in their use of the word game. Just try to read and understand virtually any contract. Over the years I have been able to decipher much of this terminology thanks to law courses and landlord contracts, but the sheer quantity and nonsense relating to lawyer-speak is daunting. One of the excuses that you might have heard about revolves around the need for precision, but I find this to be a specious argument. My programming education *(problem descriptions - facts determination - detailed instructions)* requires at least as much precision in communicating an analyst's findings to a programmer, and every-day English works just fine.

Occasionally a business entity will require that their contracts be written in conversational English, but this is a rare occurrence. And without pressure from Congress *(say, aren't most of them lawyers?)* nothing much changes. Because there are so few companies that require readable documents, I have to assume that their lawyers are arguing against that process. And there is no one in government who is willing to exert legalese oversight on businesses. As a landlord I come across rental documents that are designed more to obfuscate rather than inform. And these are the contracts that are being forced on lawyer-less renters.

Sir Francis Bacon: *"Information is power."*

While this quote's meaning may appear to be obvious, the full explanation is twofold…
-- by know something that others do not know, you have an advantage
-- obfuscate the information and you have an advantage

This gives a bit more insight into the power that information holds. Why do you think that the preponderance of our government's business is transacted unnecessarily behind closed doors, and is not often reveled to the public? Information about their activities would certainly diminish our respect for them. Say, hasn't that already happened?

White vs. Blue Collar

It's a cliché to say that white collar criminals escape their fair share of punishment. Even if they do go to jail or are convicted in civil court, their sentence is not a guarantee that justice will prevail. The original O.J. Simpson trial was a case in point. Not only did the prosecution blunder unbelievably *(the [bloody, shrunken] glove did not fit so you must acquit)*, but the Florida law allows retention of personal home equity making sure that Simpson paid minimal retribution for his subsequent conviction on wrongful death charges in civil court.

That state's real estate law is a liability-escape route that has been used by numerous felons because it protects their home's entire value from being confiscated by the courts. This is a classic example of how easy it is to buy law makers if you represent a major business interest. In this case, it was made possible by the Florida real estate folks as a way of generating more interest in Florida property by criminals. Much of their ill gotten gains can be protected there by purchasing a home.

Juries are generally more sympathetic to people of higher social standing than they are to others. Blacks far outnumber the Whites in their percentage of false convictions and severe penalties. The punishment for crack cocaine, for example, is greater than for powdered cocaine only because blacks are the major users of crack.

Juries tend to vote with their genetic-emotional hearts rather than with their genetic-rational brains because they can not easily be sympathetic to the people who have been charged with a crime or are part of another ethnic group. Emotions frequently rule the day, even though a sober, thoughtful, judgment by a jury may have been requested by the judge.

White collar crimes are viewed as being less serious then blue collar crimes which may involve violence. A person who assaults another will likely receive a harsher verdict than one who embezzles money from a company or raids a pension fund, which can causes untold anguish.

Years ago a prominent West Coast mayor was involved in the purchase of a shipping company. Then he and his equally corrupt partners depleted the worker's pension fund before filing for bankruptcy, and they suffered no jail time for the raid. Those who were due retirement payments in their old age were the ones who suffered.

Another example of a white color crime that lacked sufficient punishment was the slick wizard of junk bonds who got five years in jail for his felonious dealings. When he was granted an early released from prison, he was still a billionaire. It pays to have friends in high places, if you take my meaning.

The Kenneth Lay Affair

We all may know about the collapse of the Enron Corporation which was perpetrated by the actions of its executives. Because of their greed and the manufacturing of false fiscal reports, investors and employees lost some $60 billion dollars in equity when news of the corruption hit the fan.

While this may seem outrageous to most of us, it was eminently more tragic to those who saw their pensions or stock portfolios disappear in the blink of an eye. Can you imagine what it must be like to wake up one morning and learn that the income you have relied on for retirement had evaporated for good?

After too many years of litigation, the Justice Department finally won their cases against Lay and his associates. Justice was served you say? Well not so, because Lay died before the government recovered any of the restitution money. The appeals court then saw fit to vacate his conviction. The logic behind this reversal was that because of Lay's death, his estate and its lawyers would not have an opportunity to appeal the conviction since they did not have the benefit of a living defendant. Maybe you <u>can</u> take it with you.

This court's reasoning does have a semblance of logic. But in an effort to protect the rights of a perpetrator, they ignored the tragedy of victims. It's not as if...
-- a jury of his peers did not convict Lay
-- there had been an appeal filed for flawed court proceedings
-- there were allegations of jury tampering
-- there were suggestions of prosecutorial misconduct

None of the above occurred. But because of our court system, the Lay estate was permitted to retain more than $40 million in ill-gotten gains. So his estate kept the money because they were said to be incapable of defending against the JD's conviction. Where is the logic in that? So if you die you are not guilty, legally.

The OJ Simpson Affair

What more can be said about this despicable organism? Well the good news is that his conviction on gun charges and kidnapping has put him behind bars for many years. What kind of sick SOB risks jail time for memorabilia? The answer is that the personal power he enjoyed for years had corrupted him ultimately.

The Scooter Libby Affair

First of all, what adult would call himself Scooter? Well no matter. The real issue is that there had been talk in Washington and in conservative camps suggesting that he should be pardoned for his crime. And I have no doubt the high moral values of President Bush were easily subverted to find justification for that action.

Those who make an issue of their Godliness are just as likely to be offenders of it... or maybe more so

The logic against issuing a pardon to Libby went like this...
-- no man is above the law
-- he was convicted by a jury of his peers
-- there was no injustice in his conviction
-- people in power should not receive special privilege from other people in power
-- we should not have a double standard for those with influence

However, these arguments apparently fell in deaf ears when it came to the ultra-conservative, right-wing elements. Integrity is not as great an issue with them when it comes to protecting a member of their peer group. While this type of behavior undoubtedly served us well in our long-past tribal days, it has no valid place in our current society.

This episode should send a clear message that no politician can not be trusted to act on our behalf. So while Bush pardoned Libby in 2007 for his crimes against the American system of justice, none of the Justice Department's evidentiary proceedings *(What are the details of the crime? Why should the sentence be set aside?)* were invoked prior to pardoning. It was pure politics in play.

This action will stand as testimony that Bush, like Nixon before him, was one of the most corrupt Presidents in our history. When Bush left office in 2009, his rating was in the neighborhood of 25%... an all time low for any President. Something those in awe of him should remember.

What might learn from observing politics is that there will always be kiss-ups whose mission is to support a President's agenda and suppress evidence if asked. Like today's politics, British political history also had its Cromwells who saw it as their duty to protect the Sovereign at any cost *(but eventually it was Cromwell who took down the Crown).* These protective behaviors can stem from both real and imagines threats. From another perspective, ingratiating one's self to a superior can be highly self-serving. Keeping your boss in power goes a long way toward keeping yourself in power.

Following Precedents

When it comes to judges and courts, it is the precedents that rule the day. What this means is that previous case law verdicts dictate how judges should rule or risk being overturned on appeal. Well, you may ask, how were the first cases ruled upon if there was no existing case law to refer to? The short answer is the Kings and Queens. They and their courts made the initial judgments, and because of their power their decisions could be almost as arbitrary as they saw fit. After all who was there to object… except for the church on rare occasions?

To the contrary, some of our contemporary laws have been created by judge's rulings when allowed to pass unchallenged or were upheld on appeal. Occasionally new laws are made by the appeals courts when they strike down existing law. There are also times that laws garner new interpretations when there is a change at the bench. If a judge's legal thinking leans in a particular direction, then their judicial rulings may similarly tilt.

The law is somewhat flexible which allows judges to occasionally be attached to their own particular ideologies, just as you and I are. One positive factor that leads to judicial restraint is that the judges may find it embarrassing or their job threatened by voters if too many decision are overturned by a higher court.

These consequences may conspire to make judges reticent to create new law even when it involves a greater justice for the complainant or defendant. Oh yes, it is the legislators who are supposed to make new law, and it is the juries who are supposed to weigh the facts. A nice theory if it completely true. But the reality is that the judges occasionally do make and reinterpret laws. At times they can even nullify a juries' decision if they find fault with it.

Winning Is Everything

Many of us may have come to the false conclusion as potential jurors that the mere fact that someone has been charged with a crime amounts to two strikes against their being innocent. Couple that attitude with a whatever-it-takes-to-win mentality of a prosecuting attorney, and you have a recipe for injustice. The case against the now-exonerated lacrosse players in North Carolina should come as a wakeup call for the judicial system *(which it won't)* and for the rest of us *(unlikely, as well)*. Inertial rules.

Apparently a publicity-hungry prosecutor, who has since been disbarred, trampled on the rights of three students based solely on the dubious testimony of an alleged victim. There was no direct evidence of guilt *(DNA or otherwise)*, and there were some strong indications that the plaintiff may have fabricated her story. Had it not been for the financial resources of the three defendants, jail time could have been assured.

In another case, Michael Morton spent 25 years being innocent behind bars because he was wrongly imprisoned for the crime of killing his wife. The government prosecutor *(who has immunity from wrongdoing in office, even if it is intentional)* has been accused of hiding exculpatory evidence that would have exonerated the defendant. It had finally been revealed that Michael's son told the police it was a monster who killed his mother, and it was not his father. Years down the road, a repeat offender admitted to doing the killing. Yet this was buried and not used to release the father from jail. Eventually a coalition of lawyers and ombudsmen prevailed in this case, and Morton went free.

In 2008 the late Senator Ted Stevens was convicted in a Washington D.C. federal court on charges relating to his financial disclosers. He subsequently lost his bid for reelection. Several months later the Justice Department (*JD*) asked the judge to vacate the conviction when it surfaced that prosecutors had withheld evidence supporting Steven's not guilty plea. A released report then said that there had been systematic concealment of exculpatory evidence that would have been corroborated his claim of innocence. This Schuelke report also said that while inadvertent evidence-disclosure failures shouldn't occur, the JD meets its discovery obligations in nearly all cases. Well Mr Schuelke, *nearly all* doesn't really get it, does it? Perhaps his attitude would be different if he were the victim of overzealous prosecution.

The above cases and others like them raise several crucial points…
-- the judicial system can be manipulated by an unscrupulous prosecutor, leaving no easy way to control that abuse
-- access to money dictates how well or poorly one will be represented in court
-- there are hundreds of people being released from prison after DNA evidence has demonstrated their innocence
-- the system is far too expensive, complicated, and time consuming to be fair and balanced
-- important witnesses do occasionally die before protracted trials come to a conclusion
-- reasonable doubt is whatever the jurors thinks it is - or what they may be led to believe it is

In another case *(James Ray/ sweatlodge deaths)* the prosecution ordered the medical examiners office not to testify about their finding regarding conditions at the lodge. When this was learned through discovery by the defense and the presiding judge, the trial was in jeopardy of being declared a mistrial after months of testimony. Withholding information is unconstitutional, but the prosecution wanted to win at any cost.

Winning Is Nothing

In a three month period I received two settlement checks from class action suits in which I was *(simply by the circumstances of owning a product)* part of the class. The settlements ran well into the multi-millions of dollars for each of the cases. My shares came to 10 and 14 <u>cents</u>.

In 2011 a major bank was confronted with a class action suit for not fully disclosing the downside of interest-only home loans to the borrowers. In the settlement, the plaintiff's lawyers were awarded $25.000.000 by a judge *(being of course a lawyer)* out of the $50.000.000 that was agreed to by the defendant. After this and other expenses are subtracted, the class may see only pennies here too. It's hard to be daunted at these outcomes knowing that our laws are made by and for lawyers. How bad does our legal system have to become before we insist that it be repaired?

In another nothing case, the twenty some companies who delivered their mobile home trailers to the displaced residents of Louisiana were sued because they contained dangerous amounts of formaldehyde in their products. So a settlement was reached whereby the companies would pay fifty million dollars in fines. Why do I mention this? Because the layers take was about 50%. So for those who have or may suffer health issues, they were paid about fifteen thousand dollars each. That's thousands vs. millions! What a grand system we have.

We all have probably noticed a number of ads on TV soliciting people to various class action causes, without disclosing as much. They say things like: *you may be entitled to a monetary settlement.* Most recently they have begun to add a disclaimer that the speaker is a non-legal spokesperson. Why this change of dialog? Because there is nothing remotely legal about the ads in spite of featuring the names of legal firms.

So what should we glean from these half truths? It is apparent that the firms are doing a bit of *(currently legal)* ambulance chasing. That is, they are trying to gather as many victims *(usually of harmful prescription drugs)* as they can in order to qualify for a class action suit. When they say you might be entitled to money or some such inducement, they are merely speculating and hoping to line their own greedy pockets. By *own greedy* I mean that they have no serious empathy for their clients beyond the outrageous fees that they are given by the judges in this corrupt system.

Class actions suits are often nothing more than a vehicle for lawyers to get rich while the plaintiffs get pennies.

Supreme Principles

We would like to believe that the Supreme Court is composed of nine intelligent, impartial jurists who will make decisions that are equitable, reasonable and in accord with our Constitution. But if this were even half true, why would all Presidents be so anxious to make these appointments? The answer is that members of the court come with their own political biases, and they will be selected for having attitudes that conform to the nominating President, regardless of any faithfulness to Constitutional obligations.

While it is impossible for anyone to be completely unbiased, some of us have a greater problem with this discipline than others. Judges and lawyers are typically appointed or elected for their beliefs rather than for their impartially. Presidents are known for trying to stack the court in their philosophical favor. When a like-minded candidate is installed, reinterpretation of the constitution is possible.

Fair and balanced… a fanciful flower that rarely blossoms.

An example of agenda-peddling by the Supreme Court in favor of big business came up regarding the whistleblower legislation. The court ruled 6 to 2 that a particular tattler was not entitled to recover money for his fraud exposure because he lacked "direct and independent" knowledge upon which his allegations were based. Sounds like double-talk that was designed to circumvent an important law enacted by Congress, and which serves a pressing need.

The law was passed to penalize companies involved in illegal behavior, and to encourage those who will come forward with incriminating evidence. Do we really care how they came by their information, short of breaking and entering? The method of their discovery is hardly the point. But the Court saw fit to limit the whistleblower legislation based on a business-friendly, illogical, position. Tattlers will now have less incentive to offer their service *(risking termination for no profit),* and the offending companies will be more immune from detection.

In another decision the Court's 5 to 4 ruling overturned a long-standing ban on companies being able to set minimum prices for the vendors of their products. This price fixing scheme had previously been legislated to be illegally anti-competitive because companies could raise the price floor for their products in concert with other suppliers. In the court's ruling, price floor setting could be either competitive *(really?)* or non-competitive. So in their minds, a turn-about from the previous law was not necessarily anti-trust in nature.

Apparently the Court would have us believe that price fixing schemes can occasionally be beneficial to the consumer, but don't count on it. This decision can be seen as naked support for reduced business competition because of a counterfeit rationale. So this Court showed how easily it ends up in the pocket of big business and antagonistic to consumers.

Curiously, there is a pricing practice that has gone unchallenged for some time in the garment industry and probably elsewhere. Not only do major suppliers to large department stores dictate the décor of the selling areas that are dedicated to their products, but they may also tell those retailers what the selling prices will be, and how much and when the items can be marked down. Anti-trust? What else?

Recently I used the Internet in an effort to find the best price on a hepa *(air purifier)* filter, and discovered that every seller of a particular name brand had exactly the same price... that is every seller in the US. This universal price setting is not prima-facie anti-competitive if you believe the court.

In a 2010 Court decision: Citizens United v. Federal Election Commission it struck down a provision of the McCain-Feingold election law. That law had prohibited corporations and unions from purchasing broadcast time for election matter that named a candidate within 30 days of a primary and 60 days of a general election. This decision freed up corporations and unions to spend unlimited amounts on electioneering communications. In addition the donors were not required to be identified. The rationale behind this change was that most of this type of political spending occurs outside of contributions to a candidate's campaign, and as such the campaigns were not accountable for the veracity or lack of such with the communications. Really? What it did require is that there must be a wall between these Super PACs and the campaigns they favor. This is, of course, a flight of fantasy since that activity can not easily be controlled when it is done surreptitiously.

And there is no firewall in place which would prevent communications with candidates by Super PACs. In 2012 John McCain said "I predict to you that there will be scandals associated with this huge flood of money". The justification by the Court was that their decision was based on freedom of speech principles. Did they ever think about balancing probable corruption against the interests of the people?

The classic analogy in opposition to this ruling is the prohibition against yelling fire in a theatre. And then there is the undeniable consideration that this money will be flowing from the super rich in concert with their interests, which are unlikely to be those of the rest of us. Could the court be any more wrong-headed?

In 2006 the Court ruled that is was not illegal for telecommunications companies to cooperate with National Security Agency's warrant less eavesdropping on internal telephone conversations and email. Some 30 suites had been filed since that information became public. To its discredit, the Court upheld the previous decision in 2012.

To its credit, the Court did rebuke the Bush administration for years of stonewalling on acknowledging global warming. The EPA had presented the Court with a list of irrelevant (to *the point of being ludicrous)* reasons why they declined to take action on automobile and truck emissions. One of the more specious arguments was that auto pollution is not deemed to be poisonous. That's news to me. How about you? Maybe these deep thinkers were standing behind someone's tailpipe for too long. More likely it is that the bureaucrats owed their allegiance to the administration instead of to the public.

Then in its wisdom the EPA suggested that this matter should be resolved by a voluntary approach *(haven't we heard that nonsense before)*, rather than by regulation. I believe we know how proactive and inclined toward making changes for the better the auto industry has been throughout the years. Not!

The ruling was 5 to 4 in favor of a critical environmental issue… one that should have been a 9-zip slam-dunk. This split should make us wonder what the agenda of the opposition judges was. Perhaps the Court's philosophy is all about not restraining big businesses on whatever they deem to be in its interest, as apposed to what is in the best interest of consumers.

Gettysburg Redress

In 2012 the Court affirmed the law that allows corporations to give unlimited contributions to political parties. While the decision was not unanimous, it was unfortunate. In upholding an oblique reference to the Constitution regarding free speech, the Court ignored the damage to free politics. Their ruling was like giving all of the hotels to one of the players in Monopoly and then expecting a fair game. What it did do is give those contributors with big bucks at their disposal another avenue to corrupt the already corrupted Congresspersons.

What we end up with this decision is an inclination to paraphrase Lincoln with: Government of the corporations, by the corporations, and for the corporations. I suppose that this is not all that bad for many Republicans.

Kip's Books & Links

The books listed here are available in ebook format for Kindle™ and Nook™ readers at Amazon.com and elsewhere. Some of the shorter materials are "ideas" booklets or excerpts from longer books. Hard copy books are available at Createspace.com. The URL links, where listed, access book previews.

A BETTER BATHROOM - An Ideas Guide
Construction
https://www.createspace.com/Preview/1134187
$1.99   34 pages

A BETTER KITCHEN - An Ideas Guide
Construction
https://www.createspace.com/Preview/1134190
$1.99   36 pages

AGGRESSION & BULLYING - It's Not Just Our Wiring
Human Nature
$1.49   11 pages

AN OUTDOOR KITCHEN - The Latest Trend?
Construction
$1.49   6 pages

BEFORE STARTING HOME CONSTRUCTION - What You Need To Know In Advance
Construction
https://www.createspace.com/Preview/4136208
$2.99/$5.49   40 pages

BRAIN CHOICES & FREE WILL - Getting To Know Ourselves Using Concepts That Are Not Well Understood Or Accepted
Human Nature
https://www.createspace.com/Preview/1134191
$3.99/$5.99   78 pages

CUSTOM HOME DOs & DON'Ts - The ULTIMATE Guide To Getting Your Custom Home DONE RIGHT!
Construction
https://www.createspace.com/Preview/1134192
$6.99/10.49   266 pages

DECEPTION IN AMERICA - How We Are Manipulated Big Business, Politicians, The Press & Our Indoctrinations
Government/Business/Politics
https://www.createspace.com/Preview/1134195
$9.99/15.99   458 pages

EVOLUTION, THE BRAIN, & RELIGION - How Evolution Made Us What We Are
Human Nature
https://www.createspace.com/Preview/1134196
$4.99/$6.99   160 pages

EXCESSIVE EXECUTIVE COMPENSATION - What You Should Know About The Fleecing Of America By Executives & Boards
Government/Business/Politics
$1.49   11 pages

FOLLOWING THE CROWD - How We Fall In Line With Others
Human Nature
$1.49   14 pages

FUN WITH APPETIZERS - For Those Who Like To Entertain Well
Cookbook
https://www.createspace.com/Preview/4438108
$3.99/$5.99   70 pages

FUN WITH CARBOS - The Cookbook For Those Without A Care
Cookbook
https://www.createspace.com/Preview/4440041
$3.99/$5.99   94 pages

FUN WITH CHICKEN - The Fowl & Seafood Cookbook That Avoids Red Meat
Cookbook
https://www.createspace.com/Preview/4441007
$4.99/$6.99   148 pages

FUN WITH DESSERTS - The - What To Do When The Meal Is Over - Cookbook
Cookbook
https://www.createspace.com/Preview/4444531
$2.99/$5,49   64 pages

FUN WITH ENTREES - Getting To The Heart Of Cooking
Cookbook
https://www.createspace.com/Preview/1135491
$5.99/$8.99   172 pages

FUN WITH MEAT - The Carnivore's Cookbook
Cookbook
https://www.createspace.com/Preview/4436803
$3.99/$5.99   110 pages

FUN WITH SALADS - My Take On The Classics & Others
https://www.createspace.com/Preview/1136150
$1.99/$5.49   24 pages

FUN WITH SEAFOOD – See Food & Eat It Cookbook
Cookbook
https://www.createspace.com/Preview/4494327
$3.99/$5.99   84 pages

FUN WITH SOUP - It's Economical, & Healthy As Well
Cookbook
https://www.createspace.com/Preview/4442511
$1.99/$5.49   38 pages

FUN WITH WINE - Aging And Tasting Wine
$1.49   9 pages
An informative guide, including wine-term explanations.

GOVERNMENT FOR PEOPLE? - How the US government
"functions" without regard for the negative ramifications of its
actions
Government/Business/Politics
https://www.createspace.com/Preview/1134204
$3.99/$5.99   88 pages

HOME DESIGN GOALS - Important Considerations
Construction
https://www.createspace.com/Preview/1134209
$1.99/$5.49   36 pages

HOME GREEN HOME - The Ins & Outs Of Home Efficiency
Construction
https://www.createspace.com/Preview/1134208
$2.99/$5.49   42 pages

HOW BUSINESS FAILS US - What You Need To Know About Business Corruption
Government/Business/Politics
https://www.createspace.com/Preview/1134206
$2.99/$5.49   70 pages

HOW WE LEARN, WHY WE DON'T - Getting To Know Ourselves
https://www.createspace.com/Preview/1134212
$3.99/$5.99   86 pages

INCONVENIENT REALITY - How Big Business Shoots Us In The Foot, & How Congress And The Press Helped Get Us Into This Mess
https://www.createspace.com/Preview/1134213
Government/Business/Politics
$5.99/$8.99   190 pages

INVADING YOUR PRIVACY - What You Don't Know And What You Should Know
Government/Business/Politics
$1.49   18 pages

LAW IS FOR LAWYERS - The People That We Rely On For Our Protection Can Be The Biggest Offenders Of It
Government/Business/Politics
$1.99   22 pages

ONE POT CLASSICS - The Comfort Food & Easy Clean-up Cookbook
Cookbook
https://www.createspace.com/Preview/1134289
$6.99/$11.49   306 pages

PATHETIC POLITICS & PERFORMANCE - What We
Should Know About Our System Of Government
Government/Business/Politics
https://www.createspace.com/Preview/1134290
$4.99/6.99   112 pages

POWER BREEDS ABUSE - Or To Put This Another Way...
On Some Level, Power Always Leads To Corruption
Government/Business/Politics
https://www.createspace.com/Preview/1134291
$2.99/4.99   48pages

SELECTING A CONTRACTOR - Making The Right Choice
The First Time
Construction
$1.49   11 pages

SELLING & STAGING A HOME - Getting The Most From
Your Efforts
Construction
$1.49   6 pages

SENIOR FRIENDLY HOME DESIGN - Making A House
Safe
Construction
$1.49   11 pages

SOCIAL NETWORKING - The Downside To Exposing
Yourself
Human Nature
$1.49   5 pages

THE PRESS'S ROLE IN BAD POLITICS - What They Do,
And How They Contribute
Government/Business/Politics

https://www.createspace.com/Preview/1134295
$1.99/$5.49   32 pages

THE WAR ON DRUGS - How It Harms Everyone
Government/Business/Politics
$1.49   6 pages

TO SELL OR REMODEL - Making The Right Decision
Construction
$1.99   9 pages

TRAVEL DEALS & BARGINS – Gaming The System To Win
Travel
$1.49   14pages

www.ingramcontent.com/pod-product-compliance
Lightning Source LLC
Chambersburg PA
CBHW030704190526
45164CB00004B/460